BEHIND

AND IN FRONT

AMY CULLIFORD

A Crabtree Roots Book

CRABTREE
Publishing Company
www.crabtreebooks.com

School-to-Home Support for Caregivers and Teachers

This book helps children grow by letting them practice reading. Here are a few guiding questions to help the reader with building his or her comprehension skills. Possible answers appear here in red.

Before Reading:

• What do I think this book is about?
- *I think this book is about directions.*
- *I think this book is about what behind and in front mean.*

• What do I want to learn about this topic?
- *I want to learn what it looks like when something is behind and when it is in front.*
- *I want to learn what it means when an object is behind something.*

During Reading:

• I wonder why...
- *I wonder why students sit behind desks.*
- *I wonder why it might be important to bike behind or in front of a friend.*

• What have I learned so far?
- *I have learned that objects and people can be behind or in front of many different things.*
- *I have learned what behind and in front look like.*

After Reading:

• What details did I learn about this topic?
- *I have learned that cars are driven in lanes, and many of them are behind or in front of other cars.*
- *I have learned that classrooms have many desks that are both in front and behind other desks.*

• Read the book again and look for the vocabulary words.
- *I see the word **car** on page 3 and the word **desk** on page 8. The other vocabulary words are found on page 14.*

This **car** is **behind**.

This car is in **front**.

David sits behind.

Jordan's **desk** is in front.

Billy rides his **bike** behind.

Emily **rides** her bike in front.

Word List

Sight Words

her	in	sits
his	is	this

Words to Know

behind

bike

car

desk

front

rides

28 Words

This **car** is **behind**.

This car is in **front**.

David sits behind.

Jordan's **desk** is in front.

Billy **rides** his **bike** behind.

Emily rides her bike in front.

BEHIND AND IN FRONT

DIRECTIONS IN MY World

Written by: Amy Culliford

Designed by: Rhea Wallace

Series Development: James Earley

Proofreader: Janine Deschenes

Educational Consultant: Marie Lemke M.Ed.

Photographs:
Shutterstock: Richard Peterson: cover, p. 1; MakDill: p. 3, 14; Nikita Molochkov: p. 4-5, 14; Syda Productions: p. 6; Duplas: p. 9, 14; LeMang: 11, 14; JGA: p. 13, 14

Library and Archives Canada Cataloguing in Publication

CIP available at Library and Archives Canada

Library of Congress Cataloging-in-Publication Data

CIP available at Library of Congress

Crabtree Publishing Company

www.crabtreebooks.com   1-800-387-7650

Published in the United States
Crabtree Publishing
347 Fifth Avenue, Suite 1402-145
New York, NY, 10016

Published in Canada
Crabtree Publishing
616 Welland Ave.
St. Catharines, Ontario L2M 5V6